A Discovery Biography

Henry Clay
—◆—

Leader in Congress

by Helen Stone Peterson
illustrated by Vic Dowd

CHELSEA JUNIORS
A division of Chelsea House Publishers
New York ◆ Philadelphia

For May and George

The Discovery Biographies have been prepared under the
educational supervison of Mary C. Austin, Ed.D.,
Reading Specialist and professor of Education, Case
Western Reserve University.

Cover illustration: Bruce Weinstock

First Chelsea House edition 1991

1   3   5   7   9   8   6   4   2

ISBN   0-7910-1457-6

Contents

Henry Clay:
Leader in Congress

CHAPTER

  1 "Tarleton and the British
     Soldiers!" 7

  2 Growing Up 13

  3 The Best Kind of Present . . 23

  4 Like a Father 29

  5 "The Cock of Kentucky" . . 35

  6 Mr. Speaker 41

  7 The Peacemaker 47

  8 Home at Ashland 53

  9 Honorable Senator 59

 10 "Henry Clay for President" . . 65

 11 My Beloved Country 73

Chapter *1*

"Tarleton and the British Soldiers!"

Henry Clay scattered grain in front of his baby chicks. While they pecked it, they sang. "Peep! Peep! Peep!"

Suddenly Henry couldn't hear their peeps. A galloping horse made too much noise. An American soldier was racing down the road.

"Tarleton's coming!" the horseman yelled to Henry. "Tarleton and the British soldiers!"

Henry dropped the pail of grain. He ran toward his house. He was only four years old, but he knew the name Tarleton. That name scared the families in Hanover County, Virginia, out of their wits.

The Americans were fighting to free themselves from the British. It was 1781, the sixth year of the American Revolution. Tarleton was a cruel British officer. He stole horses. He burned tobacco fields. He captured Americans.

"Mother!" Henry called at the top of his lungs. "Mother!"

His mother stepped out the back door. Henry didn't give her time to say a word. "A soldier! He said that Tarleton's coming!"

His mother understood him at once.

"Henry, quick! Bring George and John to the house."

George and John were Henry's big brothers. George was the oldest in the family. He was thirteen. John was six. Henry knew just where they were.

He ran across the yard, across the field and into the pine woods. His brothers were picking up sticks to start the fire in the kitchen stove. Henry shouted his warning.

The three boys dashed back to their house. Sally and Molly were already there. They were Henry's older sisters, between John and George.

Mrs. Clay hurried into the kitchen, carrying her other two children. She dropped the baby in Sally's lap. She handed two-year-old Porter to Molly.

"Take care of them no matter what happens!"

At that moment Tarleton's men, all on horseback, clattered into the yard. Henry heard the commands.

"Go to the smokehouse and get the bacon and hams. Take all horses good enough for us to ride. Take saddles and bridles too."

Several men stamped into the house. "Where's your silver and gold?" one shouted.

Mrs. Clay's eyes blazed. "I have none."

"We'll find it," he said. But first the men gobbled down her fresh-baked cherry pies.

After that they searched. One man ripped his sword through the pillows.

Feathers flew! Another swung his ax and chopped off the lid of a trunk.

Outside a cheer filled the air. "She buried her treasure. We found where she buried it."

The men rushed from the house. Mrs. Clay and Henry ran faster. They saw an officer dig his sword into a new mound of dirt.

"Stop!" Mrs. Clay's voice sounded terrible. "That's my husband's grave. We buried him yesterday."

The men saw that she was telling the truth. They jumped on their horses. They raced off to raid another farm.

Watching them ride away, Henry made a promise to himself. "When I grow up, I won't let anyone hurt my family or my country."

Chapter *2*

Growing Up

A few months later General George Washington defeated the British army at Yorktown, Virginia. Cruel Tarleton never again raided American homes.

"Now we're free to govern ourselves!" Mrs. Clay told her children. Her eyes glowed. "Virginia had a glorious part in making our country free. General George Washington is from Virginia.

He led us to victory. Thomas Jefferson is from Virginia too. He wrote the famous Declaration of Independence. And never forget that Patrick Henry is from our own county. He made the speeches that roused us to fight. *'Give me liberty or give me death!'* he said.

"Patrick Henry grew up on a farm just a few miles from this house. He became a lawyer." Mrs. Clay went on telling the story of Patrick Henry. Her children had heard it many times. Only Henry was still listening when she finished.

The Clays lived on a farm sixteen miles north of Richmond, the capital of Virginia. Henry's house wasn't a log cabin. It wasn't a rich man's house either. It was an ordinary farmhouse.

As soon as Henry grew old enough, he walked to the log cabin school. He learned everything fast.

"You're the smartest one in school," his friend Robert Hughes told him. The boys were walking home one day.

"Not smart enough to learn to whistle," Henry answered.

"Can't you whistle? Start by spitting."

That made Henry laugh.

Robert looked at him carefully. "Your mouth is too wide! When you laugh, your mouth stretches from one ear to the other ear. You'll never whistle, Henry. But you laugh fine."

When they came home from school, Henry and Robert often swam in nearby Machump's Creek. Henry fished for bass with his older brother John.

He showed his little brother Porter the best hickory nut tree. They cracked the delicious nuts between two stones.

Three years of school and Henry had finished. Reading, writing and arithmetic were the only things taught there.

Now Henry studied at home. He worked on the farm. When he was tall enough, he took his turn at plowing. He held the high handles of the wooden plow. He drove the horses. Barefooted, he tramped up and down the field.

"Please stop plowing," his mother said one afternoon. "I want you to go to the mill for me."

Henry was delighted to stop. His arms ached. He threw his mother's bag of corn across the back of his pony. With that bag for a saddle he was off.

The mill was a few miles away on the Pamunkey River.

A couple of minutes later Henry heard a whistle. He laughed. He knew that whistle. It came from his friend Robert who was also riding to the mill.

The boys waited their turn to have the corn ground into flour. A group of men said hello and went on talking. The men were talking about Patrick Henry. They had just heard him speak at a political meeting in Richmond.

"His speech was great. He made my hair stand on end," one man said.

Another asked, "Will there ever again be a man who can speak like Patrick Henry?"

Henry Clay went home and hunted up old copies of *The Virginia Gazette*.

His mother saved these newspapers. They had parts of speeches by Patrick Henry. In the barn Henry practiced saying some of the lines.

After that he kept up his practicing. He made speeches in the fields and in the woods.

When Henry was still small, his mother had married again. She had more children now. The family decided to move to Kentucky.

Fourteen-year-old Henry had other plans. "I want to stay in Richmond," he told his mother. "I can work and study there. I'll take care of myself."

His mother and stepfather helped him find work in Richmond. He was promised a job as clerk in the state court. But there was no opening now.

Until there was one, Henry would work in Mr. Richard Denny's general store. He would live at the store too.

Henry said good-by to his family. He kissed his mother. "I'll ride my horse to Kentucky some day," he promised, smiling.

He said good-by to Robert Hughes too. He didn't see his friend much after that. But when Robert was an old man, he said this about Henry:

"He worked barefooted and so did I.
He went to mill and so did I.
He was good to his mama and so
was I.
I know him like a book and love
him like a brother."

Chapter *3*

The Best Kind of Present

Henry started work in Mr. Denny's store in Richmond. He took the yard-stick. He measured 20 yards of red flannel cloth for an old gentleman. Then the gentleman changed his mind. He wanted only eight yards. So Henry measured the red flannel again. He cut it. He tied up the package well.

"Too well!" Mr. Denny scolded. "You used too much string. Don't waste it!"

When a lady entered, Henry waited
on her politely. He weighed brown
sugar and green tea and black pepper.
He knotted together scraps of string.
He tied up her package.

"It looked awful!" the storekeeper
scolded. "Don't tie the string into such
awful knots. Don't waste it either."

That evening Henry walked along the
James River where sailing ships docked.
He watched a sailor splice, or join
together, two ropes without any knot
showing. The sailor showed Henry how
to do it.

The next day Henry spliced scraps of
string. No knots showed. The storekeeper was greatly pleased. "We'll save
all the scraps so you can do that. Good
boy!"

But Henry didn't feel so good. "I'm not going to spend my life making knots disappear," he told himself.

When he had time off, he walked to the Capitol building. The court was located in the basement. "Is there a job for me yet?" he asked.

"Not yet," the chief clerk answered.

"Not yet," he told Henry a few weeks later. "Not yet," he repeated a few months after that.

Henry reached his fifteenth birthday. Then the chief clerk gave him the best kind of present. "Yes!" he said.

Henry hung up the yardstick and scissors for the last time.

He dressed in his best suit. His mother had woven the cloth. It was the color of salt and pepper mixed.

The other clerks noticed right away how old-fashioned the suit was. The coattails stuck out like wings on a bird. The clerks started to laugh.

Then they saw Henry's wide smile. They saw how straight and tall he stood. They didn't make fun of him.

One day Mr. George Wythe, judge of the court, looked at Henry's work. Henry had learned all about this great man. Judge Wythe had signed America's Declaration of Independence.

The Judge praised Henry. "You write neatly. You make no blots. You do not erase."

"Thank you, sir."

Not long afterwards Judge Wythe spoke to Henry again. "I wish to write a book on many of my law decisions.

But I must dictate it to someone to copy." Henry understood. The Judge was an old man. His hand trembled so much that he couldn't write.

"Will you be my secretary?" he asked.

"Oh, yes, sir! I thank you." Secretary to the great Judge Wythe! He'd go to work for him pell-mell!

Chapter *4*

Like a Father

Henry wrote everything Judge Wythe dictated. But he let one sentence run on and on. He should have separated it into three sentences.

"Henry, how long did you go to school?" the Judge asked.

"Three years, sir."

After he heard that, Judge Wythe took time to explain the importance of words. He gave Henry a grammar book.

Henry studied night after night.

The old Judge praised him. "Your sentences are much better."

One day Judge Wythe spoke Greek. He used the words of an old Greek law. Henry's job was to write the words. But he didn't know even one letter of the Greek alphabet.

He hunted up the book in which the law was written. He copied the Greek words like a drawing lesson.

"Excellent!" the Judge said.

Then he gave Henry some advice. "Thomas Jefferson was once my student. He read, read, read. I know that every boy in Hanover County has been told to speak the way Patrick Henry speaks. I say you should also read the way Thomas Jefferson reads."

"I'd like to, sir," Henry said. The Judge opened his library to Henry. Henry began to read great books.

He never forgot the spring he was sixteen years old. "Patrick Henry is coming," Judge Wythe told him. "He will be one of the lawyers in an important court case. He's getting old. You should plan to hear him."

Henry heard him. He listened to the magic in Patrick Henry's voice. He watched the magic in Patrick Henry's face. He couldn't hold back his tears.

Three years later Judge Wythe had a serious talk with Henry. "You know my book is finished. Are you going to be a clerk all your life?"

"No. I'm going to be a lawyer." Henry had known that for a long time.

Wasn't Patrick Henry a lawyer? And Judge Wythe?

"America needs lawyers," he added.

The Judge nodded. "You must now study law with a lawyer who argues cases in court."

Judge Wythe himself made the arrangements. He talked with a lawyer named Robert Brooke. Mr. Brooke had been Governor of Virginia.

"Governor Brooke will take you as a student," Judge Wythe told Henry.

Henry tried to thank him. "I owe you so much. . . ."

Henry passed his law examination when he was 20 years old.

"It's time for me to go to that new state of Kentucky," he decided. "My family is there."

Chapter 5

"The Cock of Kentucky"

Henry rode his horse over the mountains to Kentucky. He stopped in Versailles, where his family lived.

His brothers and sisters crowded around him. But Henry's first hug was for his mother. He wrapped his long arms around her.

"You have grown tall as a giant!" she gasped. Henry was six feet one. She looked at his sparkling eyes and sunny smile. "You're still Henry," she said.

All the family laughed together.

Henry decided to practice law in nearby Lexington. It was the largest town in the state. "I rushed into a successful practice," he said gratefully later.

In one case he defended a father and son. The two men were accused of murder. Henry stood close to the jury. That jury had never seen or heard a lawyer like Henry Clay.

He thundered. Then he softened his voice to a whisper. He crouched low. Suddenly he shot straight up on tiptoe with his arms stretched high.

"I measured him with my eye. He was twelve feet tall!" one man said.

Clay won that case and many others.

Before very long he married Lucretia Hart. She was from a wealthy family.

With pride they named their first son after Judge Wythe.

Clay was 26 when the people elected him to the Kentucky Legislature, the state government. They liked his fiery speeches there.

Then the United States Senator from Kentucky gave up his job. Clay was chosen to go to Congress and finish the term. Thomas Jefferson was President.

The trip to Washington was hard. The roads were full of holes and rocks. Clay's horse had to swim across streams.

Clay found the Senators talking about a bridge across the Potomac River. Should a bridge be built or not? Clay jumped to his feet.

"Our country needs new bridges and roads," he said. He made a speech.

Clay was not only a brand-new Senator, he was also the youngest. "He should not be making speeches already!" an older Senator decided. The older man said some rude things.

Clay jumped to his feet again. He quoted a nursery rhyme. It began:

"Thus have I seen a magpie in
the street,
A chattering bird we often meet."

By the time he finished, solemn Senators were laughing.

Kentucky sent Clay back to Congress to finish another Senator's term. But Clay saw that the Senate was like a funeral compared to the House of Representatives. The House had the exciting debates.

Sometimes there was other excitement.

Once a representative objected when John Randolph of Virginia brought his hunting dogs into the House. Mr. Randolph hit the man with a cane.

Clay made up his mind. He wanted to go to the House. Kentucky elected him. ·He was only 34, already twice a Senator and now a member of the House.

Other members of the House learned that he was coming. "He's just the man to handle John Randolph," several of them agreed.

"Henry Clay is coming? Why, *he's the cock of Kentucky!*" Mr. Randolph said.

Chapter 6

Mr. Speaker

Clay was elected Speaker of the House on his first day there. That meant he was the man in charge. He sat up front in the Speaker's beautiful chair. It was covered with red and green velvet. The fringe was gold.

The House had never before chosen a newcomer to be Speaker.

Clay had a test one day soon. John Randolph entered, dressed in riding boots and riding coat. His three large brown hounds trotted at his heels. He ordered them to lie down near his seat.

"Mr. Doorkeeper!" Clay called.

Mr. Randolph snapped the riding whip in his hand.

"Keep cool," a neighbor warned.

"I am as cool as the center seed of a cucumber," Mr. Randolph answered in his squeaking voice.

All eyes turned to the young, new Speaker. He stood straight and tall. "Mr. Doorkeeper! Remove those dogs!"

It was done.

The members of the House were delighted. "Our Speaker keeps good order," one said to another.

Clay also tried to see that there was order on the seas. Great Britain was making trouble. British ships stopped American ships. American sailors were forced to work on British ships. There were other wrongs too.

"We have been insulted too long and too much," Clay said. "Other nations scorn us for taking such abuse. Great Britain is driving us to war."

The war was fought. It was the War of 1812.

President James Madison chose Clay to help make the peace treaty. Speaker Clay sailed to Europe.

"I can hold up my head now," Clay said when he returned. "Other nations respect us because we defended our rights. Our future is the brightest."

Immediately he was elected Speaker again. Then he told the House what laws he wanted. No Speaker had ever done that.

"I desire to see a chain of turnpike roads and canals from north to south. I want to see roads going west across the mountains."

"Whatever for?" a member asked.

"To bind and connect us together." Clay tossed his head and shoulders like a lion. His eyes glowed. "Our country is going to grow. I look forward to the day when our people will spread over this continent to the Pacific."

Ocean to ocean? The members tried to picture that. Why, the West was one giant wilderness! Only the Indians could live there.

Clay told the House what else he wanted. "I want laws that will help Americans to make the things they need. Who needs a hat from Europe to keep off the sun? Who needs shoes from Europe to keep out the frost? I don't want Americans to depend on others. Imagine the day when we will have one hundred million people."

Members of the House gasped. One hundred million? There weren't even ten million people in the whole country!

The House kept electing Clay to be Mr. Speaker. A poem in the Washington newspaper showed how most people felt. In the last lines Mother Nature had this to say:

"When I made the first Speaker
I made him of CLAY."

Chapter 7

The Peacemaker

America grew the way Speaker Clay said it would.

But as the country grew big, the North and the South quarrelled. They quarrelled about slavery when Missouri asked to become a state. Should slavery be allowed in Missouri, or not?

"The 22 states are like 22 furnaces in full blast at each other!" Clay said.

"Let's separate!" John Randolph of Virginia cried. "Now is the time!"

But Clay said, "Let's compromise." A compromise meant that each side gave up some of its demands. "The men who wrote our Constitution did that," Clay said. "Members of a family do that."

He made a speech on the Compromise Plan. Senators and ambassadors crowded into the House to hear him. Ladies filled the balcony.

Clay spoke hour after hour. "Let me say to the North and to the South what a husband and wife say to each other. Both of us have faults. Neither is perfect. Let us live together in peace."

When Clay finished, the ladies stood up. "God bless you," they said. Swish! Swish! went their skirts.

Mr. Randolph jumped to his feet.

He shook his long, bony finger at those ladies. *"Mr. Speaker! They had much better be at home attending to their knitting!"*

The ladies did stay at home when the speaker was dull. But Clay was never dull.

One day Clay was still speaking after three hours. The ladies wouldn't think of leaving. Would they think of eating?

Some men wrapped an orange and a cupcake in a handkerchief. They tied the handkerchief on the end of a pole. They swung the pole up to the ladies.

"Why, those men kept swinging that pole until 100 ladies were served!" one visitor reported.

But Clay did more than just make speeches for the new Compromise Plan.

He went from one representative to another, pleading for it. He worked night and day, pleading for it.

Finally the House voted in favor of the plan. Missouri became a state.

Clay was called the *Peacemaker*.

He left the House of Representatives to be in the cabinet of President John Quincy Adams. He wasn't Mr. Speaker any longer. He was Secretary of State.

Clay took with him his dream of a great America. When he sent delegates to a meeting in Panama, he told them this: "Please discuss building a canal to unite the Pacific and the Atlantic Oceans. The canal should be open to all ships of the world."

Almost 100 years later the Panama Canal was open!

Chapter *8*

Home at Ashland

When Henry Clay finished his term as Secretary of State, he went home to Kentucky. He was 51 years old.

Henry and Lucretia had a large plantation with a big brick house close to Lexington. It took its name, Ashland, from the hundreds of ash trees in the woods.

The Clay children grew up at Ashland. There had been six girls and five boys. But the family wasn't that big any more. Already five dearly loved daughters were dead. The oldest son, named with pride after Judge Wythe, was sick. He spent the rest of his life in a hospital.

The loss of his children was the saddest thing that ever happened to Clay. He had no words to tell how much he missed them.

James and John were still at home. They were the youngest sons, not quite in their teens.

"It's time we had our own race-track," Clay told his boys. They agreed! They liked horses just as he did.

The mile long racetrack was built.

There, Clay's thoroughbreds learned to race. They were trained by men who worked for him.

Some of Clay's racehorses became famous. Magnolia was one of them. Her colt, Iroquois, grew up to win the English Derby.

Clay had fine cows too. Lucretia was in charge of the work in the dairy. Cream and butter were sold to a hotel in Lexington.

When Clay wanted sheep with thick white wool, he bought a flock from Pennsylvania. The sheep walked all the way to their new home in Kentucky.

"I shall make a better farmer than a statesman," Clay wrote a friend.

Many friends visited Ashland. One English lady was a famous author.

"I like your giant ash trees," she said. "They make me feel like a dwarf."

Clay invited her to go for a ride in his carriage. "I'll show you something else that will make you feel like a dwarf."

He drove his guest to a hillside. She saw eight giant animals grazing. They raised their huge, shaggy heads and glared. Then they galloped off, bumping each other in a clumsy way.

"I don't like them!" the visitor gasped. "They're too ugly."

"That's the only herd of buffalo left in Kentucky," Clay told her.

At dinner the visitor ate the good food Lucretia served. *"Piles of strawberries and towers of ice cream!"* she said. "I like this best of all."

One day a letter came from Daniel Webster who was in the Senate in Washington. *"We need your arm in the fight,"* Senator Webster wrote. He wanted Clay to run for the Senate.

Clay had been at home about two years. He paced his favorite walk under the dogwood and ash trees. It was called *Clay's Walk.* Should he do what Webster asked? Clay knew the Senate had changed. It was now playing the leading part in Congress.

"My country needs me," he decided. "I'll go."

Kentucky elected him Senator. Clay went back to Congress.

Chapter *9*

Honorable Senator

Senator Clay and President Andrew Jackson had different ideas on what was best for the country. Clay was the leader of those who didn't agree with the President.

"He and the President wrestled like giants," other Senators said.

Clay often sucked pink and white sticks of peppermint candy at his seat. "It sweetens my temper," he said.

Before long the people of South Carolina said they wouldn't obey a law.

The law put a tax on things like cloth coming from England. Southerners had bought English cloth because it was cheaper than that made in the North. Now the tax made English cloth more expensive. This was to get people to buy American cloth instead.

"That law is unfair!" Senator John Calhoun of South Carolina said. "It makes the South poorer and the North richer." The South didn't have cloth factories, but the North did.

The North and South were quarrelling again.

"We'll separate!" the people of South Carolina cried.

"That's a terrible word!" Clay said. "Our ears shouldn't even hear it. I go for this Union as it is!"

He wrote a plan for a new law. It was a compromise. Both sides would have to give up some of their demands. That was the way they had settled their quarrel over Missouri.

Clay made a speech in the Senate on his Compromise Plan. Members of the House wanted to hear his voice again. They crowded the room until they were sitting on the platform steps and standing in the doorway.

"Heal the wounds of our country," Clay pleaded. "We want no trouble in our family. Vote for this bill."

Some Senators were for the bill. Some were against it. They had lively debates. Finally they voted in favor of the Compromise Bill. Clay's plan became the law.

For the second time Clay was called the *Peacemaker*.

New Yorkers showed how thankful they were when Clay visited their city. They tossed flowers before him. At a party some ladies took out scissors and snipped locks from his hair.

"Please leave a little or I shall have to get a wig," Clay joked.

Year after year Clay continued to be the leader in the Senate. "All he had to do was stand up," one man said. "Everybody looked at him."

It was natural that Clay's followers wanted him to be President. They had wanted this for a long time. They had tried twice to elect him, but failed.

Clay wanted to be President of his country too.

One night Clay was dining with President Van Buren in the White House. The kitchen caught on fire. A few pails of water quickly put out the flames.

"Mr. President, I am doing all I can to get you out of this house," Clay joked. *"But, believe me, I do not want to burn you out."*

Clay's followers felt sure he could be elected President this time. A friend warned Clay before an important speech. "Senator, please say nothing to hurt your chances."

Clay's eyes blazed. He shot back his answer. *"I had rather be right than be President."*

Chapter *10*

"Henry Clay for President"

"Henry Clay for President!" the Whigs shouted in 1844. They were Clay's followers. The Whigs were famous for parades with log cabins and raccoons.

Other people wanted James Polk for President. They were the Democrats.

Mr. Polk had been Speaker of the House. But Clay had been Speaker when James Polk was still a boy. Clay had been a leader in Congress for many years. "Polk? Who is Polk?" the Whigs joked.

In Ohio a boy cut down the tallest, straightest ash tree on his farm. He trimmed off the branches. He set the pole up in his front yard. Whigs were doing that all over the country.

"This is my victory pole for Henry Clay of Ashland," Peter, the farm boy, said.

"That same old coon again," his friend David teased.

In Wilkes-Barre, Pennsylvania, a visitor called at the home of Mr. Hendricks Wright. Mr. Wright had been the president of the Democratic convention that chose Mr. Polk. The visitor found the parlor filled with ladies sewing Clay banners.

"Am I at Clay headquarters? Have I made a mistake?"

"Oh, no," Mrs. Wright answered. *"Though my husband is a Polk man, I am a Clay man. In fact, the ladies are all Clay men.* If we could vote, he would have been elected long ago."

In New York City Horace Greeley said, "I want Henry Clay for President." Mr. Greeley owned *The New York Tribune* newspaper. He wrote stories telling people why they should vote for Clay. He worked so hard that he became sick.

"I'm covered with boils, 60 of them!" he said.

There was great excitement in Lexington on election day. Reverend William Gunn and his twelve grown sons marched together to the polls. They voted for their friend Henry Clay.

There was great excitement over the country while all the votes were being counted. The race was a close one. "Every hour brings a new story about who has won!" one man wrote in his diary. This went on for days.

Finally Horace Greeley had to report a bitter disappointment. "We are beaten," he told *The Tribune* readers. "Our beloved chief has been beaten."

In Pennsylvania, the ladies' banners drooped in the rain. Nobody had the heart to take them down.

In Ohio, David teased Peter, the boy who made the victory pole.

"Poor old cooney Clay,
Poor old cooney Clay,
He never will be President
For so the people say."

"Stop that!" David's father ordered. He had voted for Mr. Polk. But he told David, "Mr. Clay is a very great man. He is a born leader of men."

In Kentucky the Governor and other state officials started off to visit Clay. Reverend Gunn saw their carriages. He and his twelve sons hurried to walk behind them. Old soldiers grabbed their guns and marched along too. Many of Clay's friends joined the parade.

When Clay saw the crowd on his lawn, he came out. He started to speak. "I hoped to contribute . . . " His voice choked up. "It has been decreed otherwise. I bow to the decree."

Reverend Gunn and his twelve sons wept. Old soldiers, leaning on their guns, wept.

One man made a promise. "I'll never get my hair cut until Henry Clay is elected President!"

Thirty years later that man's hair was down to his waist and still growing. Clay was never President of his country.

Chapter *11*

My Beloved Country

Clay stayed home at Ashland. He practiced law. He raised his racehorses.

When Clay was very old, Kentucky asked him to go back to the Senate. The states were quarrelling again.

"Remember Missouri? Remember South Carolina? You were the Peacemaker," the people of Kentucky said. "Our country needs you now."

"My country needs me? I'll go."

Clay sat in his seat in the Senate, listening to the angry words. He was thinner now. He coughed a great deal.

California was asking to be a state. But California did not want the South to bring slaves there. The Northerners backed California.

"It's our right to have slaves, our right given under the Constitution," the Southerners argued. "You give us our plain rights or we'll separate!"

Clay went to work. Again he drew up a plan that was a compromise. Again this meant each side would have to give up some of its demands.

Clay was ready to tell the Senate about his plan. It was a February day in 1850. A minister from Albany, New York, walked with him to the Capitol building. Clay stopped several times to catch his breath. He coughed as he climbed the Capitol steps.

"Senator, you're not well," the minister said. "Won't you put off your speech?"

"My beloved country is in danger," Clay answered. He went up the steps.

Visitors jammed the Senate room, the halls, the street outside. They came from as far as Boston to hear Clay.

He stood up straight and tall. That was the way he stood when he was the youngest Senator.

Now he was the oldest Senator, almost 73 years old. No other Senator had seen the Revolutionary War with his own eyes. No other Senator had seen how Americans suffered to make this country their own. Clay had never forgotten that sword jabbed into his father's grave by Tarleton's man.

Clay's eyes began to burn like two suns. His whole face lighted up. "We are one family," he told the Senate. "I will try to keep us together as one family."

He spoke for three hours. Women wept and afterwards rushed to kiss him. "Patrick Henry was the only other man who ever spoke like that," men said to each other.

Clay worked hard to get his plan accepted. Some days he was at the Senate from morning until long after midnight.

"You're siding with the North," the Senator from Mississippi accused.

"I know no South, no North, no East, no West. . . . My allegiance is to this American Union!"

"You're siding with the South," a New Yorker accused.

"This Union, sir, is my country! The 30 states are my country!"

The weather grew hot. Some Senators wanted the winter carpet taken up and the summer carpet put down.

"What?" Clay asked. "Stop work from Monday to Thursday for a carpet? I say we do not stop until we get this bill passed."

After seven months the Compromise Bill of 1850 was passed and made law. There was much criticism of it. But it was what most people wanted.

Two years later Henry Clay died in Washington, still a Senator of his beloved country.

In 1861 the War between the States came. When it ended, all the states stayed together to make one great country.

"Henry Clay helped save his country until it was strong enough to save itself," one American said. Many other Americans believed that too.